It's a Dog's Life

Lessons in Assertiveness

Dr. Sparkus T. Mutt

Canine Therapist

Edited by P.V. Alvarado
Illustrations by Andrea Alvarado

Piggy Press

CAT

Canine Advice Trilogy

No. 1

158.1
A176 Alvarado, Patricia V.
     It's a dog's life: so you might as well enjoy
it, lessons in assertiveness / Patricia V. Alvarado;
Dr. Sparkus T. Mutt, seud. Panamá; Piggy Press,
2002.
     138 p., il. 21 cm

     ISBN 10: 9962-629-06-3
     ISBN 13: 978-9962-629-06-1

1. ORIENTACION PSICOLOGICA
2. ORIENTACION ANIMAL I. Título.

Any resemblance to members
of the animal kingdom,
living or dead, is purely coincidental.

TM
Piggy Press Books
www.piggypress.com

Let those sleeping dogs lie!

Foreword

Most people think that the world is going to the dogs, and they are probably right. However, if we must live a dog's life, we might as well enjoy it; and that is precisely the attitude my dog Dr. Mutt has.

Sparky, nicknamed for his sharp wit and bright sense of humor, is a seasoned mutt with years of experience in the ways of the world, which just happens to be canine.

He earned his dogtorate at the Canal Zone Canine College and did his internship as a canine therapist for the pet population near the Corozal Vet Clinic in the Republic of Panama. Now that he is semi-retired from chasing garbage trucks, he spends his time answering letters primarily from disgruntled canines who seek his advice. He calls his letters Lessons in Assertiveness, but Sparky's wisdom is universal, humorous, and even touching - no bones about it!

Sparky has graciously allowed me to edit these letters and to include them in this special collection. May they help you to come out of the doghouse and enjoy life as you should!

P.V.A.

Contents

Contents

Perseverance

Dear Dr. Mutt,

I'm a Fox Terrier, and I have a major problem. My master insists I take a bath every week! I don't mind the bath part. That feels good. It's the shampoo I can't stand. It reeks of strawberries and roses! Whenever we take our walks, all the dogs on my block make fun of me. They sniff and sneeze, and no girl dog will so much as give me the time of day.

I need help fast. What can I do?

Stinky in Seattle

Dear Stinky,

Have you tried making a break for it at bath time? As soon as you see your master coming with the rope and the hose, run and hide and don't come out until dinnertime. This might buy you a week.

Another thing you could try is to lie down and refuse to get up when he calls you, and don't get up no matter what.

If lying down doesn't work, you could shake like the dickens as soon as he wets your fur.

Or you could jump out of the tub and rub yourself all over the sofa before he gets a chance to dry you. This way, the whole family will know what that shampoo smells like.

Whatever you do, don't give up hope. Eventually he'll get the message.

Sparky

Changing Your Diet

Dear Dr. Mutt,

Help! I need a change of diet! Everyday I get the same old slop. When I agreed to leave the pound, they promised me I'd eat like a king. In fact, they even named me King.

Well, I have not had a king's ration, let me tell you! All I get is this purple stuff out of a can. I've watched them when they serve me. Their lips curl, and their nostrils flare wide. Got the picture? I only eat it because there's nothing else, and I don't want to starve.

It's been a week, and I can't stand it anymore. I'd settle for a bone once in a while. What can I do?

Deceived in Detroit

Dear Deceived,

Here are some strategies to let them know how you feel:

First, don't hurry when they call you. Next, circle around the bowl a couple of times and sniff it a bit. Then WALK AWAY. This is difficult because you're hungry, but do not eat it!

Drink lots of water that night. The next day, eat the slop, and the following day eat just a little bit.

Keep doing this for a while, and when you get too skinny, they'll bring you to the vet. He'll recommend a stable diet, and they may even spring for a steak once in a while because vet bills are more expensive than steaks.

Good luck,

Sparky

Going for a Walk

Dear Sparky,

I have a major problem. I live in a high rise, and my master works outside. Since he's a work-a-holic, sometimes he comes in real late and forgets to take me out.

Now I'm nothing special, but I need to get outside at least once a day, if you know what I mean.

Sometimes when he works extra late, I have accidents and he goes berserk. What can a poor mutt do? I'm all ears.

Motionless in Minnesota

Dear Motionless,

Well, first and foremost, you and your master need to talk. It's downright unhealthy to hold it all day long, much less half the night. Surely, he understands this.

If you're sure he really loves you, I say forget about accidents. Take the offensive. Go on the kitchen floor. If that doesn't get his attention, go on the couch. If that fails, go on his bed. Pretty soon he'll be home early every day. It should work like a charm.

Good luck,

Sparky

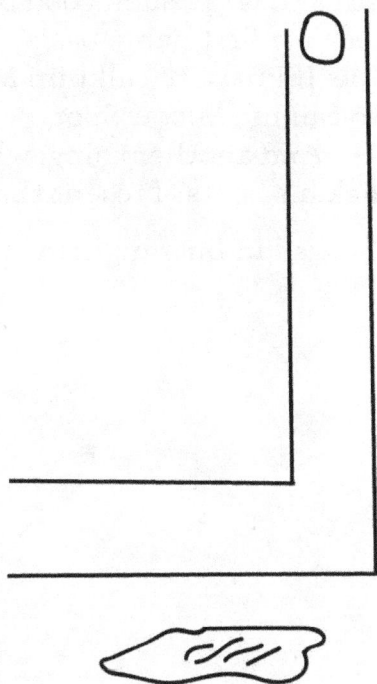

Equal Rights

Dear Dr. Mutt,

It's a well-accepted fact that we canines are man's best friends. We're there when they need us. We bark when prowlers approach. We attack on command. We fetch and carry. I know they feed us and bathe us and teach us tricks, but it's the old "You scratch my back, and I'll scratch yours" idea, and I think we got the wrong end of the stick! If we're such good buddies, why aren't we on a first name basis? This really bugs me. If I have to call him Master, I want him to call me Mister Spot.

And another thing, why should I have to lick his boots? I resent that.

Bugged in Birmingham

DOGS -R- HUMAN TOO!

Dear Bugged,

The problem lies in our basic canine-human relationship. Humans enjoy power. We canines, on the other hand, enjoy the good life. We don't get overly preoccupied about much unless, of course, somebody steps on our turf.

If you're really unhappy in your situation, you could try running away. However, I must warn you, it's a cold world out there.

Imagine a life of chasing garbage trucks and eating on the street. Think about it. Do you really need to be called Mister Spot? What difference does it make as long as you have a loving home?

If you know you're doing a good job, then be content. Trust me, that power game is not all that it's cracked up to be.

Sparky

Greedy Partners

Dear Dr. Mutt,

I have a major problem with the woman who shares my turf. She's bossy, pushy, and greedy. She doesn't like to share!

Our relationship began about five years ago. I was a homeless vagabond, literally abandoned by an abusive master. I roamed the streets for days until I spotted this cute little number with a snappy bark. She let me stay, and one night has turned into five years.

I admit we cuddle a bit on stormy nights, but that's not the problem. What bothers me is that if I'm two minutes late for dinner, she wipes my dish clean! And lately she snaps at me while I'm eating! I can't take it anymore! She's a born fighter, and I'm not. What can I do? Help me, please.

Desperate in Denver

Dear Desperate,

First of all, get hold of yourself. Reflect on your past behavior. Keep a journal of your daily activities for a month, and note her reactions. Circle the negative ones and see if there is a pattern.

This should give you some insight on how to handle her moods. Maybe she doesn't like your daily jaunts. About her eating your dinner, try hanging around until after dinnertime and then going for your walk. Invite her to go along. You may be pleasantly surprised.

Good luck,

Sparky

Riff-raff & Ruffles

Dear Dr. Mutt,

I'm fed up. I'm from a long line of French poodles. According to my aunts we have always been pampered, but I'm sick of it. We have a standing weekly appointment at Sarah's Salon on 44th and Carlyle, and my mistress insists we keep it. But just once I'd like to skip out and run free. I want to cut loose. I want to feel the wind in my fur without these tight little ribbons and bows.

We live in the penthouse of the Watts Building, and on sunny mornings we dine on the balcony. Groups of young dogs, some much younger than I, roam the streets. They appear to be having a grand time sniffing wherever they please.

Today one rather rakish fellow barked at me. Of course, I blushingly barked back, but my aunts were furious at his audacity and forbade me to answer him again. He didn't wait long because there was a girl in the group, and she nudged him away.

What torture! When I mentioned how I feel to my aunts, they said these dogs are riff-raff and beneath my station and that I am destined for a grand life. Well, I don't feel grand. I feel trapped by tradition and haute couture. What can I do?

Rebellious in Rochester

Dear Rebellious,

First of all, don't despair. Look at the facts and work from there. You feel trapped. Since you live in a high-rise, escape is extremely difficult but possible; and since your aunts keep tight reins on you, you'll have to plan carefully. The way I see it, you have only two options. One is quite dangerous and could lead to perdition. The other depends on the mercy of a servant.

Plan A:

Wait by the door a few minutes before the maid takes out the garbage. When she opens the door, slip quietly out BEHIND her.

If she uses the stairwell, follow her. These stairs usually lead to the ground level, and perhaps you can make your escape then. The danger here is that you may not be able to come home.

Plan B:

If the maid uses the elevator, sneak in BEHIND her and hope she lets you ride down. Since her arms will be tied up with the garbage, she won't be able to grab you right away.

Be nice to her. Lick her boots. Cry if you must. She may feel sorry for you. When the elevator doors open, dash to the front door and whimper. She may take you for a walk.

Plan B is by far the safer option, but whichever you choose, good luck.

Sparky

No Can Do

Dear Dr. Mutt,

My master opened the gate today, and my friend and I headed for the garbage cans down the street - our usual run. Well, it was anything but usual. There was this new guy on the block, a Rottweiler, and he thinks he owns the neighborhood. When my buddy and I arrived, this guy wouldn't let us near the cans.

He was bigger than both of us combined so we decided to give it up. This really burns my bananas! I'm only canine, and I don't like being humiliated. How do we prevent this from happening again?

Down in the Dumps

Dear Dumpsters,

You were smart to back down because a conflict with one of these guys will get you nowhere. However, you need to ask HOW did the Rottweiler get out? Normally these guys are kept under lock and key.

I guess you have no control over your escapes, but I would venture to say that the Rottweiler will NOT be loose again, so rest easy.

If it does happen again, play it smart. Follow your instincts and back down. Better to be boneless than battered!

Sparky

The Prodigal Pup

Dear Dr. Sparkus,

My master brought me home only a week ago, and already I'm in trouble big time. It all started with our daily exercise program. My master runs every day, and he insists on dragging me along. Since his nose is so high off the ground, he can't smell the wonderful aromas in a dog's world such as freshly bagged garbage and newly piled compost heaps. He sprints around corners and along fences with gay abandon while I am condemned to race alongside without a moment's rest! I can't even stop to answer a friendly bark!

Well, last night as he dashed uphill, I headed downhill. The chain broke and I bolted. And then, I was in paradise. I never knew there were so many girls in my neighborhood, and I have a date with all of them the next time I get loose, which takes me to my present situation. When I came home, garbage bag in tow, the gate was locked! I felt betrayed. I barked, but no one came so I waited in the cold, wet garage. Early this morning the master's mate opened the gate and let me in, but there was no warm and friendly welcome, no breakfast biscuit waiting. What have I done wrong? Where did I go astray?

Punished in Paradise

Dear Punished,

You hit the nail on the head with GONE ASTRAY. No can do, Buddy. If your master wants you to jog, you jog. If he wants you to walk, you walk.

There are very few things you have a say in. On occasion, he may set you free to roam at will, but this comes only with great trust. And if you should ever break that trust, it's difficult to convince a master you're worthy. And forget about presents! It's an inexplicable phenomenon, but for some strange reason, garbage bags don't soften a master's heart.

My advice to you is to sit it out, and play it cool, but whatever you do, don't poop on the patio.

Sparky

The Chair

Dear Dr. Mutt,

I know we canines are supposed to be the kinder, gentler breed, but giving up my place to a feline is passed the limit.

Actually, it's a question of seniority, a respect for rank, so to speak. The trouble started a month ago when my mistress brought home her nephew's cat, and the house hasn't been the same since. Ferdinand was only supposed to stay for a week, and anybody can take living in the rough for a week; but it's been four weeks since Ferdinand arrived, and we literally fight like cats and dogs. I can't stand him.

Besides, he's a snob. He sits properly at table, doesn't slobber when the food arrives, licks his paws before he eats, and doesn't piddle on the rug. And he sits in my chair! That's right! My chair! And to make things worse, he does it on purpose because he only does this on Saturday night when he KNOWS I watch football. What can I do? I've held my patience in check long enough!

Peeved in Providence

Dear Peeved,

You're right to be peeved. Whoever heard of a cat taking precedence over a dog? Then again, we must be prudent in our observations. There may be humans, and even canines, who think that felines are a superior race! Tis sad but true, and this is a hard bit of news to swallow; but then again so is life.

We canines must show the world that we are superior! So what if felines sit in our chairs? So what if felines traverse our paths? Felines can't bark! We must act unified and dignified, and forgive the injustices caused us by the world of felines. Not to worry. Humans love us, especially man. Truly.

Sparky

Back Seat Blues

Dear Dr. Mutt,

I'm not one to complain, but lately life has dealt me some pretty hard knocks.

It all started when my master bought his new car, a sparkling red jeep with large windows, my favorite kind.

Well, yesterday he invited me to go for a joy ride, but he took along a new friend. I've ridden shotgun for years, and this time, I thought, would be no different. How wrong I was!

You can imagine my dismay when this newcomer sat up front, and my master, my BEST FRIEND, laid newspaper on the back seat and then tied my chain to the bars above the window! I barked, I squirmed, I jumped, but to no avail. He only had eyes for her.

Then to make matters worse, he lowered the window only a tad. I couldn't lean out and take in the fresh air! Well, you can imagine, with all the driving up and down hill and turning right and left and no fresh air, I got car sick.

It was humiliating. The girl friend gave me the dirtiest look, and my master said things I'm not sure I can forgive. What can I do? I don't want to sit in the back again, ever!

Belittled in Bellington

Dear Belittled,

Take heart. Perhaps this female is just a passing fancy, so play it cool. Lay low for a while. If your master invites her to the house, be nice; but don't go licking her feet. She may not be a canine lover.

Give the guy some time. He seems like a nice fellow. You said you ride shotgun, and not many canines get that far in life. Be patient. He'll come around. We're not called man's best friend for nothing.

Sparky

Thin-skinned Willie

Dear Dr. Mutt,

I'm a canine with extremely sanitary habits. Even though my master forces me to live on the patio, I avoid the grass at all costs. On our daily walks, I stick to the sidewalk. Why, you may ask, do I do this? Well, I'm allergic to grass. It makes me break out! And the other reason is pure and simple. Ticks and fleas live in the grass, and I can't stand the itch!

Why is it that we canines must endure the infestation of such pesky little creatures? Not only are they bothersome, they are devious and malicious! They don't stop at a simple nip like a mosquito. They dig in and hide in places unreachable by the canine paw, no matter how much I scratch. It's very disheartening. What can I do?

Ticked off in Topeka

Dear Ticked,

Don't give up hope. You're not alone in the fight. In fact, there is a documentary TV program called "The Fleas in America, a Tick in Time Saves Mine," which airs monthly on the Canine Broadcasting Network. I'm a faithful viewer. Did you know that ticks can't swim? This is only one bit of information you can learn by watching.

The question is, do you have access to this program? Since you live on the patio, you are at the mercy of the master. Hopefully, he is a sympathetic human who realizes the importance of good health and will give you an occasional dip on the wild side.

Here are a few activities to draw attention to your situation: Scratch like crazy. Lie on your back, roll back and forth and groan. Whenever he calls you, don't respond; whimper and hide. Let me know how things work out.

Sparky

Look Both Ways!

Dear Dr. Sparky,

I should have trusted my mom's advice. From the time I was just a little mutt, she cautioned us pups to look both ways before crossing the street. Well, I didn't, and now I'm paying the price.

It all happened when my master left the gate open - something he never does. I should've known better than to blatantly venture forth, but the scent was so enticing that I sniffed my way out the yard and into the street. I don't remember much after the horn blast, and the vet says I should be grateful to be alive. I guess I'll be wearing this cast for a few more weeks. The itching is maddening.

So Dr. Sparky, I want to warn all my canine buddies: Look before you sniff!

Plastered in Peoria

Dear Plastered,

Too often we go off thinking that the world has been created for us alone. How mistaken we are! Thanks for sharing your experience.

And to all you impulsive characters out there, take heed. Don't be a blind sniffer!

Sparky

Patience is a Poodle

Dear Dr. Mutt,

It is not my custom to write to advice columnists, but here I am. I need help. For weeks now I have been scoping out this cute little French chick who lives next door. You wouldn't believe how cute and dainty she is. Her soft, curly white fur is tied up in little red bows. Her paws are petite and painted, and her name is Patience.

I realize I don't have a pedigree, and my family name is Mutt, like yours; but gee, Doc, I'm a nice guy. I've done everything and more to get her attention. I've howled to the moon, barked like mad, and hopped as high as I could. Everything the guys say I should do, I've done; all to no avail. Why I even risked strangling myself by pulling my master in her direction. She didn't even look at me. I'm at the end of my rope. What can I do?

Praying for Patience

Dear Praying,

First off, you're trying too hard. These foreign gals are in a class by themselves. You need to play by their rules, and sometimes for us regular guys not even this will get us a calling card.

They like attention, subtle attention, a glance in her direction, maybe a slight bark or two. But no whimpering! This is sure to scare her and her master.

Give it another shot, but don't kill yourself in the process. If it doesn't work out, consider a platonic affair with Patience and look for someone else. There are a lot of lonely hearts out there.

Sparky

Walk, Don't Balk!

Dear Dr. Mutt,

Something is fishy at my house. When I called my roommate out for our usual jaunt, he seemed reluctant, almost angry. I patiently sat while he searched for his sneakers. Then he spent another ten minutes putting them on. Then, if this doesn't beat all, he actually jerked my chain! Then he yelled at me in front of my friends because someone pooped on the sidewalk, and he found it.

Boy was I angry. Where's the appreciation? Where's the respect? Here I am doing him a favor. It is my walk, and I go rain or shine. I only let him come along because he lives at my house.

We've been roommates for a long time, but I'd like a bit more respect. What do you think?

Resentful in Raleigh

Dear Resentful,

Man is infinitely less patient than we are. Who among us would think to get angry over something so insignificant as stepping in poop? Your master has obviously never tried rolling either. I fear, however, that the problem goes beyond poop.

You mention the sneaker episode. This sounds like a delaying tactic to me. I've seen it many times at my own house. What was the weather like? Was it rainy or cold or both? Man does not appreciate inclement weather. The only ones I know who forge ahead in all weather are the mail carriers. Your roommate probably came home in a bad mood, and he took out his frustration on you. It sounds like he needs a friend so give him another chance. And on your next walk, lead him around the poop.

Sparky

Early Risers

Dear Dr. Mutt,

I like to sleep late, and these early risers really bug the daylights out of me! I can understand barking at the occasional cute little female, but what is it with the garbage truck? Barking will not stop these guys from doing their work, so what's the point of waking up the whole neighborhood? Can't a fellow get some rest?

Drowsy in Detroit

Dear Drowsy,

You're not alone in your misery. Unfortunately, there is something innate about barking. It seems that since ancient times we canines have shown our prowess by barking at anytime at anyone and at anything that moves, and that includes the moon!

So may I suggest that you quit bucking the system. Hit the sack earlier and greet the day with the rest of us. You'll be a happier camper, I assure you.

Sparky

Picnic Shmicnic!

Dear Dr. Mutt,

Yesterday I experienced my first, and hopefully my last, picnic. "Picnic, picnic, picnic! We're going on a picnic!" was all I heard from Rick, the little boy child that brings me my food. Naturally, I was curious as to what this picnic thing was. Never in my wildest dreams did I imagine how humiliated I would be. Not even being chased by a Rottweiler could compare to this. The household stirred before the garbage trucks passed, and we packed into the car and set out before sunrise. I was lucky to get a window seat next to Rick. He and his siblings kept chanting that picnic refrain, and thankfully the wind roared though my ears as we headed toward our destiny.

If I had known then what I know now, I would never have ventured from my sleeping mat. It was a comedy of errors, actually. We set up a make-shift table on the ground: table cloth, cutlery, the works. Rick told me to guard the goods while he and the others explored the area.

Nothing much was happening so I decided to do some exploring of my own. That's where I made my mistake. I should never have left my post. I literally sniffed my way into the doghouse, as the humans so disrespectfully call humiliation.

I'm ashamed to admit it, but I got lost! I couldn't find my way back to the picnic, and Rick and the others had to come searching for me. I was so embarrassed, and what's worse is while I was AWOL, some bears got into the goods. I don't ever want to go on a picnic again.

Humiliated in Huntsville

Dear Humiliated,

Don't take these things so much to heart. You were in unfamiliar territory, and from what you tell me your nose was probably affected by all that ram-air from the window. Come to think about it, you were lucky. In Bear v. Dog fights the bear usually wins, and don't worry about any picnics in the near future. Rick and the others don't want to deal with bears either.

Glad you made it home in one piece.

Sparky

Blue Moon

Dear Dr. Mutt,

I'm so depressed. I thought things couldn't get any worse, but they did. I left home at a very young age. I followed my nose and was lost before I knew what had happened, and the streets have been my home ever since.

It hasn't been a bad life, really. Oh, there've been the occasional scuffles with packs, but I'm street-wise. It's just that yesterday I was having lunch near the garbage cans in the park, and this cute little mutt was showing these humans the sights. As they strolled by, our eyes met, and I was thunder-struck. I tried to follow her, but the humans wouldn't let me. They called me every name in the book, names that I wouldn't repeat to my sainted mother.

I'm trying to look on the bright side, but it's the dark side of the moon I see. I'm so lonely. I want a girl friend.

Belittled in Bossier City

Dear Belittled,

All humans aren't like those humans, believe me. However, we need to focus on you.

If it's that particular girl you'd like for a friend, you probably need to clean up a bit and hang out in the park.

If she's a regular park-goer, you'll see them again. When you do, let them pass by. Then follow them at a distance to find out where she lives. Under no circumstances should you let the humans see you, and maybe you could talk through the fence after the humans go to bed.

If that doesn't work, there are many lonely canines in this world; and the park is a great place to meet someone. Life is tough, but take heart!

Sparky

Thunder & Lightning

Dear Doc,

I live with this cat who never gets rattled over anything. I mean there could be a monsoon outside, and Fritz is cool.

As for me, well, I'm ashamed to admit it, but thunder and lightning scare the living daylights out of me. Am I weird or what? I need to know.

Shaking in Shadow Grove

Dear Shaking,

It's a known fact that lightning comes before thunder; and the proximity of the lightning is determined by the time measured between the sight of the lightning and the sound of the thunder.

We canines have this innate sense of timing where we can actually warn people about the disturbing effects of thunder by barking furiously after a lightning bolt. If you think you tremble at thunder, you should see how bent out of shape a human gets!

Actually our barking prepares them for the big blast of sound from the thunderbolt. We are rendering a service to humankind.

There is nothing to fear from lightning or thunder so quit shaking. Just don't stand under any trees during a rainstorm.

Sparky

The Dark Ages

Dear Dr. Mutt,

I don't know where to begin. If I had known what lay in store for me when my master invited me for a ride in the truck, I would have run away from home. I thought we were going on a routine visit for a rabies shot, but it was all over before I knew what happened.

Now my friends say it's too late because I've been neutered. I'll never be able to, you know, have puppies! Why did this happen to me? When I wake up, I'm so depressed that I can't even bark. Don't we have any sayso in our lives?

Despondent in Dallas

Dear Despondent,

There are so many reasons for what humans do, but we canines are not always privy to that information. It has been said that they neuter us to keep our population low.

This explanation, though cruel, sounds like a reasonable one. They're afraid we'll take over the world, a feat we could easily accomplish.

You are a victim, but you can help others in the fight for canine rights. Your wounds will heal; and when they do, you can spread the word to forewarn others against this vile treatment of canines. Knowledge is power!

Sparky

Moving Again

Dear Dr. Mutt,

Today I found out we're moving - again! This is our third move in a year. I'm tired of establishing new turf every three or four months. It's hazardous to my health! At our last place, I had to defend myself against one German Shepherd, a Beagle and three Poodles.

What is it with these humans? Why can't they settle down?

Temporary in Tucson

Dear Temporary,

I think humans share part of their ancestral history with canines. I know for a fact that we canines were nomadic during our distant past, and humans would sometimes tag along for safety. This is probably why the canine-human bond is so strong to this day. Perhaps this is also the reason some humans continue the nomadic tradition, as do some of our canine relatives.

As for your situation, depending on how attached you are to your master, I would recommend that you either focus on the positive aspects of each new location or get a new master.

Good luck,

Sparky

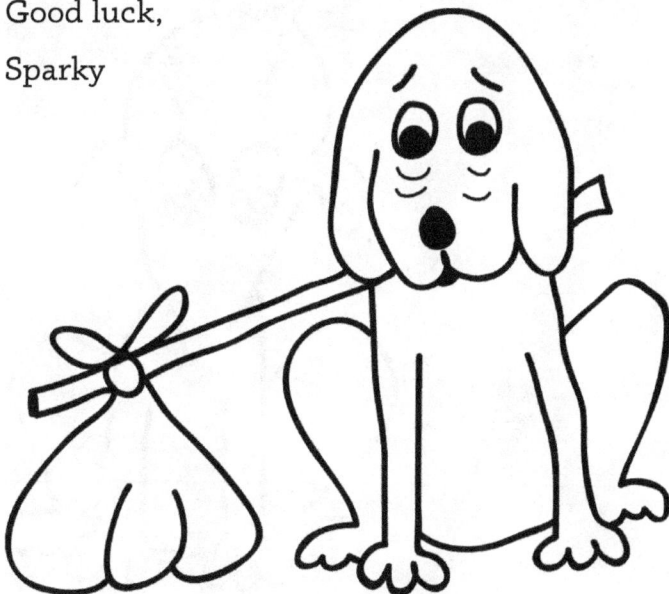

Pie in the Sky

Dear Dr. Mutt,

Today I found out that I'm really a nobody. My life has been a lie. Since I was a little pup, I was told that I was the best of the best. I've trained with the greatest and dined with the finest. This was the biggest contest of my life, and I didn't even place!

I was so humiliated I couldn't even wag my tail! How can I show my face in public again? Where did I go wrong, Sparky? Tell me how to lift myself out of the dregs of life.

Dreary in Dayton

Dear Dreary,

One contest? Are you talking about ONE contest? Does your whole life depend on one contest?

Life is much more than one contest! So what if you didn't place? Does this make you a failure? Get a grip! Don't let one little contest set you back! You're young, and there will be many more contests, believe me, so don't judge yourself according to another's criteria. What's most important is how you see yourself.

Don't allow one insignificant competition to set you back. Be proud of your canine heritage, and don't worry if humans can't appreciate it.

Be of good cheer!

Sparky

New Year Nausea

Dear Dr. Mutt,

That blasted time called THE NEW YEAR is here, and the night sky is framed in fireworks.

I can't eat, I can't sleep, and I dare not venture forth for fear of my life. Every boy and his father are setting roman candles to make Nero proud.

It's worse than the 4th of July! I would be okay if my master would let me sleep inside, but no way. All I can do is hide under the bench on the patio and whimper. It'll take me a month to get over the shivers. What do you advise?

Trembling in Takoma

Dear Trembling,

What can I say? Humans like noise - the louder the better. Have you ever listened to what they lovingly call music? Is it any wonder that we howl?

If you're feeling extra daring, try howling with the explosions. If not, you'll just have to bear with it. Stay close to home, and keep your head covered. What you can't see may not hurt you.

Sparky

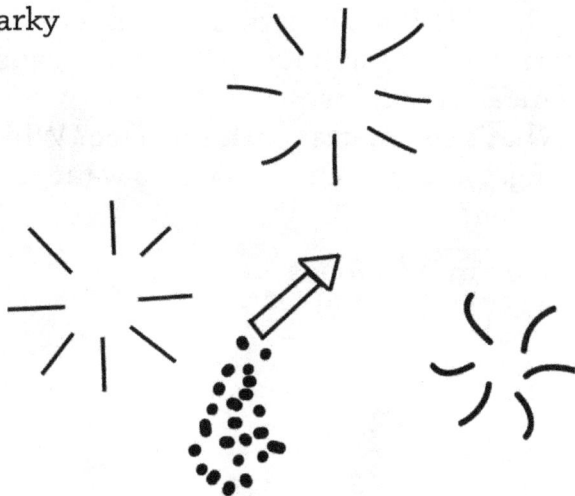

Bewitched & Bewildered

Dear Doc,

I'm despondent. I'm three years old, and still I can't get a date.

Yesterday I hiked over to the local dump and spotted this chick who lives nearby. I trotted over to say hi, and she growled at me. I was stunned.

To make matters worse, a group of older guys were watching me. One of them told me to get lost, and two others chased me to the hole in the fence. I'm lucky I'm fast because they meant business.

What's the matter with me, Doc? Why can't I get a date? Why don't girls want to talk to me?

Bummed in Big Woods

Dear Bummed,

Chalk this chick off to experience. Here's a little fatherly advice from an old dog:

1. Always check out the neighborhood before you approach.
2. Once you've scanned the area, be cool. Walk in like you own the place, and stake out your own territory. Most canines will respect that.
3. Puff up your chest and wear your tail high. Girls seem to notice this.

Practice your moves around the yard till they become second nature to you. Then venture out. Most of all, though, THINK POSITIVE! You're only three. You have your whole life ahead of you, if you're lucky; and you seem to be. Let me know how things work out.

Sparky

Buried Treasure

Dear Dr. Mutt,

Yesterday I escaped under the fence and headed toward the park where the action is. On my way, I discovered the biggest bone I've ever seen. Of course, I couldn't stop right there and feast. It would've taken me all night. So I brought it home and buried it in the flower bed thinking I'd work on it little by little. However, when I returned to the spot, my treasure was not there!

I don't want to point paws at anyone, but I find it suspicious that Floyd, my yard mate, was chewing on a bone mighty similar to the one I buried. He's bigger and older than me. What can I do to get my treasure back?

Fleeced in Frankfort

Dear Fleeced,

Probably nothing. Like you say, Floyd is bigger and older than you are. Anything you do to antagonize him may result in bodily harm, a situation you want to avoid at all costs. All I can suggest is to learn from your mistakes and not bury your treasures where Floyd can get at them.

Sorry about your loss.

Sparky

Iguana's a Goner

Dear Dr. Sparky,

Picture this: Palm trees swaying gently overhead, birds chirping across the sky, and cats nowhere to be seen - a tropical paradise. I was nodding off for my usual little siesta before dinnertime when the ruckus began. Barking, growling and hissing filled the air. When it was all over, there lay a dead iguana four feet long! I never saw it coming, and if I had, I would've looked the other way.

I feel so bad. This mutt I live with is such a show-off. She attacked and killed a member of an endangered species, and she feels no remorse! To top it off, she never shares. She is so heartless. What can I do? I can't stand her!

Perturbed in Panama

Dear Perturbed,

Report her to your local environmental authority. Even though it's too late to help that iguana, it may not be too late for your yard mate. If it's true that iguanas taste like chicken, she may attack again. She needs counseling, pronto!

Good luck.

Sparky

Tyrannosaurus Vexed

Dear Dr. Mutt,

I've been maligned. Yesterday the EPA came by my house and issued a warrant for my arrest. They claim I killed an endangered species, but they've got it all wrong. I was the one in danger. There I was minding my own business in my own yard when this giganitic dinosaur came at me. I had seen him lurking in the trees overhead for the last few days, and I had already decided that I'd give him a wide berth. But when this huge guy crossed my path, he bared his great big teeth, flexed his sharp claws, and whipped his long tail. He hissed at me, and the giant plates on his back whiffled back and forth. What was I supposed to do? I was so scared that all my natural canine powers took over, and that's what saved me. It was a hard fight, and I don't regret it. I don't even want to think of the alternative.

I'll admit I've had my share of scuffles, and I've taunted a few here and there, but this guy came on my turf! I had to defend myself, and that bozo who shares the yard with me didn't lift a paw to help me. This is so unfair! Why do they want to lock me up? I deserve a medal for bravery. I don't want to be tied up for life. It wasn't my fault. Help me, please!

Imprisoned in Panama

Dear Prisoner,

There are two sides to every story, and it's always good to get the underdog's point of view, if you'll pardon the expression. Your situation is a touchy one.

The EPA is a powerful organization that tries to help the animal kingdom, especially an endangered species. Unfortunately for you, the iguana fits in that category. It does resembles a dinosaur, but dinosaurs are extinct so forget that defense! The fact that it came on your turf and threatened bodily harm may be your saving grace.

For the next few days, if I were you, I'd be the sweetest, gentlest puppy in town. Humans prefer our company to a lizard's any day. And be careful of what you say in front of your yard mate. I don't think he has your best interest at heart. Keep me posted, no pun intended, sorry.

Sparky

Necktie Party

Dear Dr. Mutt,

What is the point of wearing a collar? Fleas and ticks crawl under and bite at will, and those critters know where to hide. I scratch, but to no avail.

The other day I nearly choked to death when I tried to slip through the fence. Lucky for me my master came home early and unhooked me. I've tried pulling the blasted thing off, but it's too tight. You'd think my master could take a hint. I don't see him wearing one. In fact, no one in the whole family wears one. What can I do?

Choked in Chattanooga

Dear Choked,

I have some good news and some bad news. The good news is that your collar brings status. It identifies you as someone's personal canine. Without your collar humans would think you were homeless, and the authorities would haul you away.

The bad news is you have to wear it forever. Try to look on the bright side. Wear your collar with pride, no matter what it looks like. Think of it as a crown of glory because without it, you're nothing but a stray.

Sparky

Un-hip!

Dear Dr. Sparkus,

Yesterday was the worst day of my life. I dug my usual escape under the fence and was marking my trail when out of the blue my left hip gave out. I couldn't move an inch. I tried in vain to lift my leg, but it wouldn't move. I circled around the hydrant and tried the other side, but I couldn't put weight on my left leg to lift my right one.

I was only five minutes into my routine, and to make matters worse two of the best looking girls on the block watched in horror.

I am thoroughly humiliated. How will I ever live this down? Is there a remedy? Can I be cured?

Liftless in Laughton

Dear Liftless,

Before I can give you any advice, I need to know your age. If you're older than ten human years, you're pushing your luck by digging under fences just for adventure.

It sounds like a pulled muscle or a torn ligament, so my advice is to stay inside the yard for two weeks to allow your leg time to heal. If by then you still can't mark off your territory, seek professional help. Surgery should be your last resort.

Oh, and don't worry about the chicks. Once you're up and about, you can tell them it was a war wound. They'll eat that up. Let me know how it goes.

Sparky

Of Mice and Mutts

Dear Dr. Mutt,

I'm a feline and I have a bone to pick with you canines. I know we've never seen eye to eye, but there have been moments in history where we have shown tolerance.

A case in point. Today, after breakfast, my housekeeper had fluffed my pillow, and I was snuggling into dreamland when a squeaky clatter intruded upon my slumber. I lifted an eyelid to make certain it was not a mouse. But no, it was the miniature pinscer who inhabits our flat. As usual, he barked incessantly. I tried to stare him down, but to no avail. The boy child offered him biscuits, and this calmed him; but he broke into such a racket once he'd finished. To my relief the girl child carried him off to the den.

I am not a complainer, but my rest is sacred. To me, this canine is nothing more than a rat that barks. He should beware.

Ruffled in Rangoon

Dear Ruffled,

We canines do thrill at the simple things in life, and this could be a case of youthful exuberance.

Did you ask the young sport why he was barking? Contrary to public opinion, canines bark for very good reasons - most of the time. There must have been something wrong for him to keep up the racket after the biscuit. You'll never know unless you inquire. Hopefully, he'll mellow with age. Give him a chance.

Sparky

Getting Trashed

Dear Dr. Mutt,

I'm a good dog. My master tells me so every day, but this time I think I'm in big trouble. You see, we just moved into this neighborhood, and we don't have a fence. I shouldn't have left the yard, but the night was young and the spirit of adventure was strong. So I sniffed my way to perdition. Before long a powerful aroma captivated me, and I followed my nose to the garbage can on the corner.

I know I shouldn't have done it, but the flesh is weak. I stood on my hind legs and pushed over the can. By the time I finished, there were cartons all over the place. I tried to clean up the mess, but there was only so much I could do so I came home.

Nobody knows who did it yet, but it's only a matter of time. Why do I feel so guilty? It was a gourmet's delight.

Fed Up in Fenton

Dear Fed Up,

Give yourself a break. There's something about a resting garbage can that is irresistible. We've all been there. Be prepared, however, for a prison-like atmosphere if you become a prime suspect. It could mean a week or so of solitary confinement.

Humans are strange like that, but thankfully they have short memories.

Sparky

The Call of the Wild

Dear Dr. Mutt,

I was born and raised on a farm as was my daddy and my grand-daddy. However, the master sold the farm and moved to the city last summer. Now we live high above the ground, and I hate it. I have to sleep on a mat on the balcony, and we go for walks at night leashed together. I can't chase rabbits or flush birds from the bushes, and the horns are driving me crazy. Everybody blows signals that don't make any sense. They're weird.

I'm so sad. I miss the farm. I'm from a long line of hound dogs, and hunting is in my blood. What can I do?

Depressed in Dayton

Dear Depressed,

It has been said that the only thing constant in life is change, and life changes constantly.

Focus positively on what's happening around you. Being leashed together can be fun. Work with your buddies, and make your walks a joint venture. Pick out a different scent each night to explore as a unit.

City life, with all its drawbacks, can be as exciting as a hunt on the farm. There are only two rules for survival, however: stay alert and don't poop on the sidewalk.

Let me know how it goes.

Sparky

Canine Vegetarian?

Dear Dr. Mutt,

I'll get straight to the point. Can dogs be vegetarians? For the past few weeks I've been unable to eat my food, which I know is gourmet because of the cute little puppy on the can. But lately I've been getting these terrible stomach pains, and for some strange reason I'm attracted to the grass that grows along the sidewalk. It's like I'm in a trance. The grass calls me. I have to eat it. But once I do, I get real sick and throw up. Then I feel much better. Then I eat again and have to run for the grass.

What's happening to me? Am I a freak or what?

Going Crazy for the Greens

Dear Going Green,

Don't despair. All you probably need is a change of diet. When you start eating grass, that's your body's way of saying "Hey, buddy, you've eaten something bad so let's get rid of it before it makes you really ill."

Lay off the gourmet stuff for a while if you can. Of course, if you venture out and consume such delicacies as frogs, toads, lizards, or snakes, then you're in for real stomach trouble. No amount of grass can help you there because some of those fellows are downright poisonous. So stay away from them.

As for becoming a canine vegetarian, anything's possible, especially with the help of your master. But I wouldn't worry about it. Just drink lots of water and exercise daily, and you should be feeling better soon. Take care of yourself.

Sparky

Not Vain Just Glorious

Dear Dr. Mutt,

I just want to make a statement. Humans think I'm cute, or at least that is what I have been told all my life. So why not take advantage of my gifts? Being cute is a talent like any other, right? I'm a model, and my latest assignment was a shampoo contest. The winner receives a lifetime supply of shampoo. Well, my neighbor, who I might add smells like a garbage can, gave me the hardest time. She called me an "Air Head."

I am not vain. I do not seek glory or praise or anything of that nature. I just like to be in the limelight! It's fun. It's different. It's not routine. Why, then, do others criticize me for posing for advertisements?

Annoyed in Annaheim

Dear Annoyed,

Jealousy makes us do crazy things. Not all of us are endowed with the same number of gifts, and some of us have to "make do" with much less than a generous portion. Usually it's the "making do" that is difficult, and probably 90% of the canine world is "making do," no pun intended.

So take heart, be of good cheer, and have a good word for your neighbor. Not to worry.

Sparky

A Rose to the Nose

Dear Dr. Mutt,

I'm in the doghouse, literally. Usually I get to sleep in the kitchen, but not today. Heck, it's not like I did anything bad.

Joe, my master and I were out on our usual jaunt in the park, and he let me off my leash so I could run and do a bit of exploring. I always come back when he whistles, and today was no different except that this time I struck gold. I found some perfume and rolled in it. I was so proud, but I knew something was wrong as soon as I got close to Joe and wagged my tail. He was definitely not pleased. In fact, he tied me up and hosed me down as soon as we got home. Now I'm confined to quarters till who knows when.

This perfume is a real "girl grabber," Sparky, a literal "cat's meow" if you'll pardon the expression. What's wrong with Joe? Where did I go wrong?

Aromatic in Arlington

Dear Aromatic,

Your first mistake is to assume that humans have the same olfactory senses as we canines. Supposedly humans use to be like us, but over the centuries, they have lost their senses. I have heard there are groups of humans in distant parts of the world who still practice our ancient aromatic customs, but I am not sure of this. Obviously, Joe does not have a canine's gourmet nose, and you'll have to get used to it or spend your life in the doghouse.

Sorry.

Sparky

Monkey Business

Dear Dr. Mutt,

I'll keep this brief. I live on a wildlife reserve where the animals tend to roam free - that is - all except me! I'm supposed to be a watchdog, but more often than not I am used as a beast of burden, and this is no ordinary burden I'm talking about either. I have to carry the monkey back and forth. You read right. A monkey!

It all started when I first arrived. I was just a young pup, and this chimp was nothing more than a baby. He would jump on my back, and I would carry him around while he held on for dear life. All in good fun! Everyone thought it was so cute. Well, what began in fun has turned into a chore, and I'm sick of it. Every morning that monkey jumps on my back and refuses to get off until I pack him across the yard.

I can't stand it anymore. I don't want to hurt the guy, but I'm desperate! What can I do?

Ridden in Rockefeller

Dear Ridden,

Walk only when you absolutely have to, and sleep next to your food dish. Just stay put. When you do walk, if the chimp hops on your back, sit down and stay there until he gets off. If you do this often enough, he may get bored and stop.

This is called TRAINING. Whatever you do, don't try to out-run him, he'll think you're playing with him, and you'll have to start the training program all over again.

This is a hard one to shake, but with patience you may be able to get this monkey off your back.

Good luck,

Sparky

A Tail of Woe

Dear Dr. Mutt,

Yesterday I was in heaven. Today I'm nowhere near the pearly gates!

It all started after the rain stopped. There was a soft spot near the corner of the fence, and I did what any mutt would do. I dug out and spent the night on the town. Garbage cans were overflowing, and I hit every one! Such delicacies the heart could not imagine!

Before I knew it, the sun caught me by surprise. I was on my way home when I spied my master's car at the stop sign. I approached the window eagerly to hitch a ride home. Instead of the usual cheerful reception, he shouted and made angry faces. So I waited it out. These tirades never last long. He finally opened the passenger door, and I hopped in.

That's when it happened. He slammed the door on my tail! Never in my life have I felt such pain. I'm ashamed to admit it, but I cried. He took me home, locked me up in the garden and didn't give me a second glance.

Now I think he did it deliberately. It's been a week, and all I've gotten is the usual K-rations - no specials. And worst of all, my tail is bent! What can I do to straighten it out?

Crooked in Crampton

Dear Crooked,

Short of plastic surgery, your looks have been changed forever. Be positive, though. You can use that crook in your tail to your advantage. The gals tend to admire a roguish look. The pain will subside with time.

Sorry,

Sparky

Jet Setter

Dear Dr. Mutt,

I'm an Irish Setter, and I had the most horrible experience of my life. My master accepted a new job across the country, and we flew to our new home.

When he first talked about this transfer, I was so excited. I have always dreamed of travel. Well, no longer.

My enthusiasm frosted over when we got to the airport. My master flew inside the cabin, and I went CARGO! It took me three days to thaw out, and I thought I'd never be able to eat again! Slowly, however, I've gotten back my land legs, and my appetite has returned.

Just thought I'd share. Traveling is not all it's cracked up to be.

Crated in Cargo

Dear Crated,

The big question: DID YOU GET FREQUENT FLYER MILES? If not, then no amount of discomfort is worth it! Until we have our own Canine Airbus, we're at the mercy of our masters.

Sorry you suffered,

Sparky

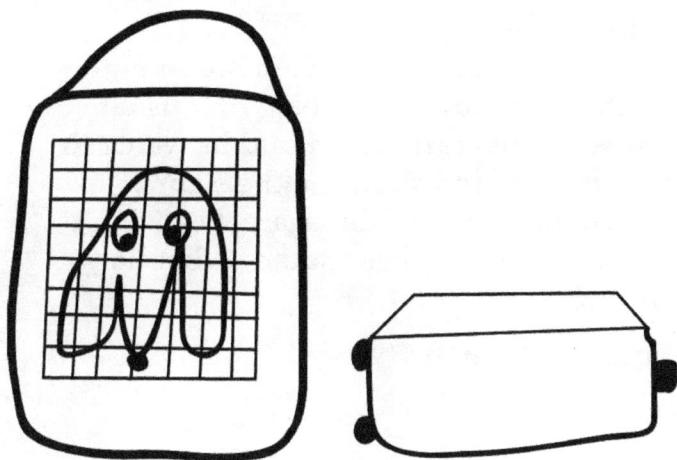

Down Under

Dear Dr. Sparky,

We just moved to a farm in the outback of Australia, and I am amazed at this place. It's very much like the ads. Adventure abounds! Why only last week I was out exploring when I met this young Aussie canine. We chatted for a while, but it was difficult to understand him because he barks with an accent!

His name is Dingo. He is rather cute in a wolfish sort of way. Not your usual domesticated canine. He said he wants to take me out and show me the sights.

I'd like to meet him again, but I don't want to be a one-night stand. What do you think?

Prudent in Perth

Dear Prudent,

If you're in for adventure, then dance with the dingo. However, if you're looking for a long-time relationship, don't go to him; make him come to you. Things tend to boomerang when we're perilous. Be patient, and learn to speak the dingo lingo.

Good luck,

Sparky

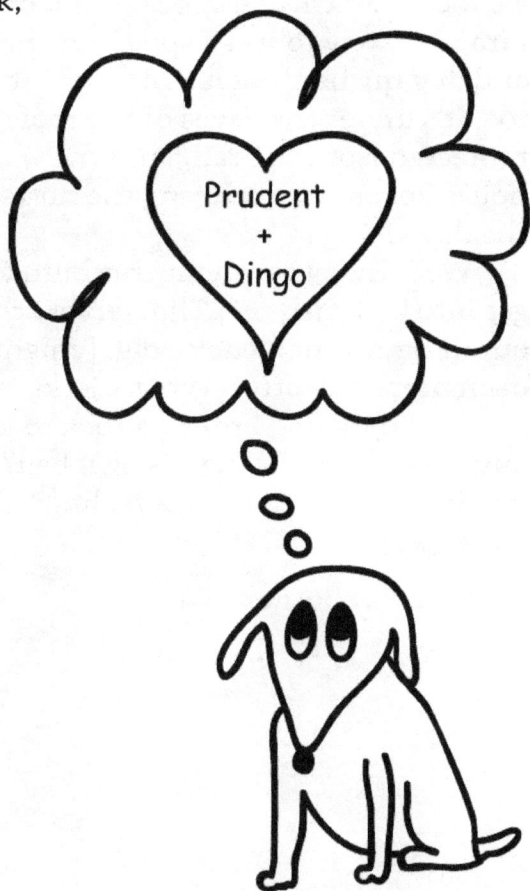

Prudent
+
Dingo

Bed Rock

Dear Dr. Mutt,

I've had it with this guy who shares the yard with me! He's an unmitigated bum! Since our master is an environmentalist, he provides us with our meals; but we have to fend for ourselves in the yard. Recently, we moved to this new locale, and of course I immediately found a spot near the house and dug my bed. Such a nice spot it is, too. It's under the eaves of the roof so it's protected from the rain, and the wall of the house keeps it cool during the hottest part of the day.

Well, the other night this bum tried to get into bed with me! The nerve! I threw him out. If he had helped me dig, I might have been more receptive. What a jerk!

This morning I rolled a rock to keep him out. Why didn't he dig his own bed? He's got two fore paws. I don't like feeling this way, but what can I do?

Bolstered in Bordertown

Dear Bolstered,

It's obvious you don't care much for your yard mate's lazy habits, but you must have a soft spot for him. Not in your bed, of course, but in your heart. Otherwise, you wouldn't feel bad.

How long have you known him? Was he like this before you moved? Did you tell him how you feel? Does he contribute in other ways, perhaps?

Try to make him understand that cohabitation is a two-way street. Invite him to dig with you; don't snap at him. Since humans arrange many of our domestic relationships for us, it would be beneficial for you both to get along. You don't have to be a pushover, but if you get rid of the rock and move over, you'll be better off. Be a good sport. Otherwise, the yard can be a very lonely place.

Good luck,

Sparky

Don't Fence Me In!

Dear Dr. Mutt,

Since my master and I live alone, and he doesn't believe in taking walks, I'm left pretty much to myself behind the fence. I do have a view of the street, though, so I can communicate with other canines. At first it didn't bother me to see the guys and gals passing by. We'd bark and laugh and race back and forth along the fence, then they'd go on home.

My problem began yesterday when this cute little gal strutted by, and my friend Spot, who lives next door, was following her. I tried to get him to bark and race along the fence with me, but he never stopped. Then a bunch of the other guys ran past the fence.

I tried to get them to tell me what was going on, but they were in too much of a hurry. About an hour later, I could hear everybody hollering and having a good time. I dug desperately to get under the fence, but the base is cement and I ended up cutting my nose and scraping my paws. Then I tried to jump it. Big mistake. I nearly hanged myself. I wanted to go to that party so bad! What can I do? My yard seemed so big. Now I feel left out and lonely.

Frustrated in Franklin

Dear Frustrated,

I know it's not enough to say be thankful for what you have - one square meal and a place to sleep. Life behind a fence is difficult to bear in the best of times, especially when we see others with so much freedom. I can tell you for sure though; the party season won't last too long.

So be patient. Your friends will be stopping by again to chew the fat through the fence.

Sparky

Tick Sick

Dear Dr. Mutt,

My master has me de-ticked at least once a month, but it never fails. As soon as we get home, those pesky little creatures are waiting to ambush me. I'm not allowed inside the house so no matter where I make my bed, they find me. There's no place to hide. I spend my days rolling and scratching and my nights moaning and twitching.

Fedora the Feline told me they carry disease. Is this true? What can I do? I'm sick of these ticks!

Ticked in Thomasville

Dear Ticked,

Fedora is right. Ticks do carry disease, and they can make you deathly ill. Sometimes a change of diet can help.

Have you ever heard of a "Salty Dog?" Well, you must become one. Add salt to your diet. This will make the ticks stop biting.

Also, you might try a pod of garlic a day or some brewer's yeast. This may give you bad breath and a bit of gas, but at this stage, who cares, right?

I don't know how you could communicate this information to your master, though. The only suggestion I can make is to sleep near the door jamb. Ticks like to travel. If they crawl under the door, and your master finds them in the house, he may call the local bug man to come and spray the yard. This would give you some relief. Once a month is not enough. He should remove the ticks more often.

Hope you get help soon,

Sparky

No Place Like Home

Dear Dr. Mutt,

I've been homeless all my life. I never knew my father, and I don't remember my mother. I saw myself once or twice down at the pond in the park where I go for a swim, and to tell you the truth, I'm not half bad looking.

Well, the other day, I was rummaging for my supper in this pretty posh neighborhood when the strangest thing happened. As I was trotting along the fence, this fellow barked at me, and of course I barked back just to be polite. Then I stopped dead in my tracks. It was like looking into a mirror. There I was staring at my double. The other fellow was equally surprised because he barked like crazy until his master came out. Instead of shooing me away like usual, this human opened the gate and let me in! Then he called out the mistress and the kids. They talked to Spot, and he told them I may be his lost brother. So they fed me and bathed me and bought me a collar! They even gave me a place to sleep!

I'm dumbfounded. Could Spot really be my brother? Are humans that generous?

Doubled in Duluth

Dear Doubled,

It's possible that Spot may be your brother, but family is not defined by blood alone. Humans, like canines, can be very generous, and many care deeply about our problems. However, taking in strays is not an everyday occurrence.

You are one lucky dog! Congratulations. Enjoy your new found home and family.

Sparky

Fifteen Minutes *of* Shame

Dear Dr. Mutt,

The other day I was on my usual rounds and found myself in the middle of a major public function. How was I to know that the world's cameras watched as I sniffed, searched and found a place to go! What an embarrassment! Now my friends accuse me of lifting my leg to the world. I am so humiliated. How can I ever live this down?

Mortified in Metairie

Dear Mortified,

Don't fret! Government officials around the world have done worse than lift their legs in public. Take heart. Unless you run for office or belong to someone important, you have nothing to worry about. What you did was perfectly natural.

Sparky

Pick of the Litter

Dear Mr. Sparky,

I have three brothers and two sisters. They are bigger than me. They make fun of me. Spot called me a runt. I barked at him. Fred wouldn't let me eat so I tried to bite him. Mom fussed at me. I'm sad and hungry. I'm little. What can I do?

Tiny in Toronto

Dear Tiny,

Don't worry about being called runt. Names don't make the dog. If your family lives with humans, bark when they come around. Lick their fingers. Nip at their toes. Nuzzle their legs. Humans like that and will think you're cute. Whatever you do, don't let Fred or anybody else stop you from eating. Fight hard for your food. It's important. You may not grow real big, but you will grow up. You will be okay.

Take care and don't cry,

Sparky

Rockin' & Rollin'

Dear Dr. Mutt,

I'm not your usual canine. I'm a rocker. We all know that one of the most efficient ways to keep our teeth clean and healthy is to chew on bones. However, my master refuses to invest in bones so I use what is available - rocks!

It's not as bad as it sounds. Instead of playing with bones, I find rocks in the street and carry or push them home. Then I chew on them. As a result, my teeth are quite pointed, and my friends call me Cave Dog.

Rocking in Rochester

Dear Rocking,

Necessity is the mother of invention, and bad breath can destroy your love life. Better to have pointed teeth than halitosis! Besides, pushing rocks is great exercise! Just don't swallow when you chew. That could be bad for your digestion.

Sparky

Yogi Dog

Dear Dr. Mutt,

I live in a tiny apartment overlooking the city. My master works shifts and is often too tired or sleepy to take me for a walk so my big problem is exercise, or rather the lack of it. I know how to use the remote for the television so I don't get too lonely.

Well, the other day I was watching a special on the benefits of Yoga. I tried a few of the stretches, and I especially like the cobra position, the alternate leg pull, and the down dog. These are naturals for me. I have difficulty, however, with the alternate nostril breathing, but I'm determined to lick it. I feel much better already, but I'd like to try some more advanced postures. What do you suggest?

Relaxed in Reno

Dear Relaxed,

Yoga is a wonderful way to relax. I have been greeting the sun since I was a pup, and since humans copied most of the positions from the animal world, you shouldn't have any problems advancing.

As with any exercise, however, it is always best to take things slowly. Be super careful with the locked lotus position. Never attempt it alone. You may be sorry.

There's an excellent book that I use called Hum in the Morning - Howl at Night by Krishna Dog. If you have access to the Internet, you can write to him at yogicanine@godog.com.

Have a good day,

Sparky

William Didn't Tell

Dear Dr Mutt,

The other day my master invited me to an open-air concert in the park. I felt honored by the invitation because not many canines are included in these events. We arrived early and found a spot on the hillside with a commanding view. The maestro took his position, the crowd settled, and the music began. It was wonderful. All was going well, and I was howling along to the beat. Then all of a sudden, there were cannon bursts! It was like World War III!

I broke from my leash and beat a path home. I don't know what time my master came in, but I hid in the safety of my little house until the sun came up.

What I would like to know is why did they have to ruin a concert with cannon? I think that will be my first and last concert.

Deafened in Deridder

Dear Deafened,

I couldn't agree with you more about the cannon. Why ruin beautiful music with explosions? I've said it before, and I think it bears repeating. Humans love noise. It must have something to do with the shape of their ears.

Sorry about the concert.

Sparky

A Nose *by* Any Other Name

Dear Dr. Mutt,

I'm a Federal Agent and have a trusted position at an international airport. My nose is worth its weight in gold. My job is to smell the luggage for anything unusual.

Today began like normal. My boss and I headed out for the luggage carousel with me in the lead sniffing the ground carefully. When we arrived, the cases were already tumbling down and circling around Carousel 4 so I put my nose to the task sniffing each waiting passenger.

Nothing seemed amiss until this little old lady crossed my path. Bells and whistles sounded in my head. Alert! Alert! So I did what I am trained to do. I grabbed her purse and began to pull, but she wouldn't let go. I pulled and growled, and she pulled harder and growled back! Then she began to strike me with her umbrella! I was so taken aback that I let go of the purse in stupefaction. She let loose a tirade of insults at my boss and me that are not permissible in polite society.

We accompanied her to the office and had her open her purse to check out what she had stashed away. To my humiliation, all we found was a ham and cheese sandwich and a pickle from the flight.

How was I to know? I could have sworn it was drugs. This is my first big mistake. Now my boss is giving me funny looks, and I'm ashamed to walk the concourse. What went wrong? How will I ever live this down?

Snuffed in Seattle

Dear Snuffed,

Though canine noses are famed for their accuracy, we all make mistakes, some bigger than others; it depends on the nose. It was probably a cross-wind or something. No one can say that you shirked your duties or that you were lax on the job. You should feel proud that you erred on the side of righteousness and in the line of duty.

So relax and thanks for keeping the airways safe for travelers.

Sparky

Who is that Doggie?

Dear Dr. Mutt,

My master Jack and I sit in the den every evening after dinner to watch TV. It's our quiet time. No one bothers us.

Well, last night during a commercial, I noticed a shadow cross the window. Of course, I immediately went to investigate. To my surprise, it wasn't one of Jack's friends. It was a strange dog. He was tall, dark, and rather rakish. His big pointed ears and long snout reminded me a bit of Clark Gable and Mr. Spock. Our eyes met only for a moment before Jack came to the window, and the stranger ran away.

I couldn't sleep all night wondering who he was, what he was doing by my window. Well, this morning after Jack left for work, the stranger returned. He smiled at me through the window. I tried to open the door, but Jack had locked it. The stranger stayed by the window all day until Jack came home and shooed him away. Jack was so jealous. He even called me the "B" word!

I'm distraught. I've never felt this way before about another dog. What's happening to me? Am I being disloyal to Jack to want to run off with a total stranger?

Dazed in Daytona

Dear Dazed,

Certainly not! It's perfectly natural and normal to be attracted to our own kind. The canine-human relationship has a long and rocky history, which dates back to the days of cave dogs. We've guarded humans from themselves for ages. Jack is not really jealous, he's just afraid to watch TV alone, and perhaps he's also concerned about your well-being. What do you know about this stranger other than the fact that he's good-looking and persistent? If you run off with him, will he be there in the morning? If you get "in the family way," will he stay when you need him? If not, will Jack take you back? Ask yourself these questions before you run off and leave the comforts of Jack's living room.

I'm not saying don't go; I'm saying think twice and be careful.

Sparky

Who Needs a Kiwi?

Most Honorable Sparkus-san,

I hope this letter finds you well, and long life follows you. I am Shotoko Shiba Inu. My ancestors were great Japanese farmer dogs. Of course, I do not live on a farm. My honorable master Kyoto-san is a salaryman here in Tokyo. We live in a modest apartment building on Harujuku Street. He knows how much I love to run so Kyoto-san and I go for long walks every day after work.

Though he is a wonderful master, I am distressed. Yesterday he brought home Kiwi-san, a parrot. Kyoto-san said it was to keep me company during the lonely day. It would be okay if this bird were quiet, but all this bird does is talk, talk, talk! How can I make that bird shut up? Please help me.

Troubled in Tokyo

Dear Troubled,

About the Kiwi, I suppose you could ignore it and it may get tired. But the chances of that happening are pretty slim to none. I hear that parrots are polyglots so the only feasible solution I can think of is to teach it to converse in Canine. Begin with simple barks; then work your way to phrases then complete sentences. This could be a long process, but well worth the effort. Once Kiwi learns Canine, you could explain to him how you feel. You would be killing two birds with one stone, so to speak. Your days would be filled with challenge, and Kiwi could become your friend.

Thank you for the good wishes. I wish the same for you.

Sparky

Tricks Are For Kids

Dear Dr. Mutt,

I've had it with humans and their Pavlovian theory! I am a wolf from the Yukon. I was captured, literally lured away from my mother with a piece of salami by some human scientists when I was just a pup, and I have lived under the light of experimentation ever since.

But enough is enough! To quote my favorite French philosopher Albert Canine, "Je refuse!" No longer will I salivate at the sound of a bell just for a cookie! And if I must jump through hoops, I expect worker's compensation! In fact, everyone should unite in the B.O.W.W.O.W. (Bark Out Wildly With Other Wolves) effort to liberate all canines from human bondage! Bark if you know what's good for you!

Thanks, Dr. Mutt, I just had to vent!

Nettled in Novgorod

Dear Nettled,

How did you get from the Yukon to Novgorod? Just wondering.

Anyway, I agree with you that we should not denigrate ourselves for cookies or peanuts or anything of the sort. We must be proud of being Canine. Serving humanity, however, is part of the price we pay to make the world a better place. What's a cookie here and there if you don't compromise your integrity?

Just remember that we can do what they can do but better, but they don't need to know that. It's sufficient that we know.

Peace,

Sparky

P.D.A.

Dear Dr. Mutt,

I'm all in favor of being affectionately demonstrative, but there are limits to what is acceptable social behavior and what should be reserved for the privacy of the doghouse. Today my master and I were on our usual afternoon stroll in the park, when lo and behold as we rounded the bend, two young mutts were making out near the lake.

My master, bless him, just laughed; but I was so embarrassed, I didn't know where to turn. What's the world coming to when our youth are so unabashedly loose and disdainful of the proper social morés?

Shocked in Shreveport

Dear Shocked,

You hit the nail on the head with LOOSE. Obviously, these young mutts are foot-loose and fancy-free. They have no guidance. Their masters, if they indeed have any, seem unconcerned for their welfare.

But you needn't be shocked at their decorum. It's a dog's life, and they will learn quickly enough the ways of the world.

Sparky

Cats Are People Too!

Dear Dr. Mutt,

My cats, Spots the Bengal, and Cinnamon the Siamese, want to know why dogs get all the favorable press, while cats are always the villains. You have Lassie, Rin-Tin-Tin and Sparky. We have Sylvester, the doofus bad guy always lusting after Tweety-Bird.

I'd like to know why cats always get a bad rap in the press?

Stumped in South Florida

Dear Stumped,

If you ask me, I would say that dogs are true politicians (sans corruption), and cats are not. Dogs play up to the people. I may even go so far as to say that dogs are Democrats, and ... No, I'd better not go there.

Suffice it to say that it is a simple question of personality - dogs are extroverts and cats are introverts; dogs are hams and cats are not; and the press likes a ham.

To be honest, canines, though rather gauche and slobbery, are naturally friendly; while felines are more independent. Now I KNOW cats CAN be nice, but do they truly WANT to be? Who can tell? Cats are so self-assured that they appear not to NEED anyone, whereas, dogs ARE NOT and DO.

But please tell Spots and Cinnamon that it takes TWO to tangle (tango?) and what would life be like without cats and dogs? Hope this answers your question.

Sparky

P.S. To be fair, we do have Goofy!

A Ticky Situation

Dear Dr. Mutt,

I don't want to sound like I dislike folks who are different from me, but I have this problem with our new neighbors who moved in next door. The people are OK, but the horses are covered with ticks.

Dog bug season is more outrageous than ever this year, and it's because the horses brought more than their share of these annoying arachnids into the neighborhood. The dogs down the street are also concerned about it, but what can we say or do without sounding like we're narrow minded?

Bitten at the Beach

Dear Bitten,

Our equestrian brothers are built to bear burdens. It's in their DNA. And of course, they can't scratch like we can. All they have are their tails, and some don't even have that! So they are pretty much doomed to carry whatever hops on their backs, ticks included, and to go wherever they are led. They came with their masters so just give them a wide berth and don't go barking at them from behind. Their kick is worse than your bite!

Sparky

Down the Road

Dear Dr. Mutt,

My master and I have had a spat. I wanted him to walk with me, but he told me he was too tired. So when he opened the gate to give me a biscuit, I ran off. I thought he'd follow me, but it's been two days, and he hasn't come to get me. He knows where I am because the last time I ran away, he came with a leash and brought me home. I'm beginning to worry. Suppose he doesn't come for me? There's not much to eat around here, and it looks like rain. What should I do?

Depressed and Dirty near the Dumpster

Dear Depressed and Dirty,

Go home. Use your nose, and smell your way back. Be mature and responsible. He might fuss at you a bit, but he'll be happy to see you and he'll forgive you. Masters are like that. No matter how cranky they seem, they love their dogs. So put your tail between your legs and go home!

Sparky

Military Mutt

Dear Dr. Mutt,

I have a big problem. It's my dad. He's a career military guard dog, and you know how those guys are! There's nothing like the armed forces. He never stops barking, "Son, the military has given us our meat and potatoes!"

Potatoes, indeed! I hate potatoes! I've just been weaned and now he wants me to enlist! I don't want to be a guard dog. I want to study archaeology. I know I'd be great at it. I can dig a hole faster than you can fetch a stick, but HE wants me to follow in his paw prints. Help me, please! What can I do?

Traumatized in Travis

Dear Traumatized,

Get a grip. Your dad wants what's best for you, obviously. The military has been good to him, and he rightfully is proud of his military career. After all, he is serving the nation, and being of service is the noblest of careers. It's the canine way.

Though archaeology is interesting and useful, perhaps you could find a happy medium. There are many branches of the canine military. Maybe your digging talents could be useful in the forensic department, for example. Anyway, there are worse things than joining the military.

Good luck,

Sparky

Bean Bag Bed Shred

Dear Dr. Mutt,

I blew it. My master came home the other day with this great big old cushion, and he put it outside right on the patio. He said it was for me! I was so excited that I claimed it for my own right away. Imagine, a real bed!

But after supper, when I crawled in ready for a relaxing night, something didn't feel right. It was too round so I grabbed one end and shook it back and forth hoping to fluff it out. But that didn't work so I sunk my teeth in deeper and shook harder. But no luck! Then I dragged the thing around the yard a bit to soften it up, but it got caught on the rose bush, so I tugged real hard. I heard a little rip, but by the time I got it loose, the cover was in shreds, and the yard looked like a snowstorm!

I tried to put all the pieces back together, but I kept gagging on those little foam pellets! When the master came out for his newspaper, he called me a lot of names I'm not too happy about and said I'd have to sleep on the ground for the rest of my life!

It's not my fault the bed tore. I was just trying to get comfy. Help, please, how can I get another bed?

Grounded in Gutenberg

Dear Grounded,

Humans are pretty generous for the most part, but when it comes to being charitable, they don't appreciate ingratitude. And I must say, though your bean bag bed wasn't that comfy, shredding it wasn't very wise. A little prudence might have saved you from a hard dirt bed.

Be patient. It'll probably be a while before your master feels sorry for you again, but he might come around. Especially if it really snows in Gutenberg!

Good luck!

Sparky

Doberdog Duo

Dear Dr. Mutt,

Yesterday I took the master's wife out for a jaunt around the neighborhood. There we were with the wind in our ears, minding our own business, just having a grand old time getting our exercise when all of a sudden, these two Doberdogs launched a ferocious attack, snarling, snipping and snapping ugly remarks at us. I stood my ground, of course, neck fur hirsute, ready for anything. But I must admit that if it hadn't been for the ten-foot hurricane fence, they would have had the master's wife for lunch! The funny thing is though that within seconds after they began their rampage, they began arguing with each other, and then the real fun began. We laughed all the way home, albeit a bit shaky from the experience.

But one thing concerns me. I shudder to think if these guys had not been behind bars. Why can't they laugh and bark at the sunshine and thunder like the rest of us? Why are they so bitter with the world?

Dumbfounded in Diablo

Dear Dumbfounded,

We are the products of our upbringing so don't let the foibles of others get you down. That poor duo is doomed to dwell within the confines of a very big cage, and I can imagine their vocabulary. I'm sure if they had gone to a different school, they would not have acted that way.

You are a very lucky dog! You have a master and a master's wife who understand the concept of freedom. Enjoy it and try not to rub it in when you pass by the duo's house again, just in case.

Sparky

Newspaper Knucklehead

Dear Dr. Mutt,

My master is a newspaper nut. He loves to read the newspaper and always wants to be the first one to read it. This would be okay if he left the paper in order, but he dumps each section randomly as he reads, and the rest of us have to wait for him to finish and then try to figure out which end is up! It's really frustrating, so the other day, when the newsboy threw the paper into the yard, I asserted my individuality and read the paper first. My only problem was the wind. By the time I finished the last section, the yard was dotted with newsprint. I tried my darndest to collect the pages and place them in order, but to no avail. So I put the paper together as best I could and left it neatly on the doorstep. Now I've been quarantined to the back yard until further notice.

What I want to know is why I'm being punished for doing what the master does every day? It's not fair. I have a right to the news, too!

Limited in Limbo

Dear Limited,

You are fighting the good fight, but I suggest you give it up. Even though we are on an equal footing with our human counterparts when it comes to intelligence, they think they are smarter and want first dibs on reading the newspaper. So for world peace, I say let them read the paper first. Who cares in which order you receive it? It's all news.

My advice to you is to deliver the paper and let him read it first. When he's done, then it'll be all yours, and you can devour it or toss it all to the wind if you choose.

Sparky

Senior Citizen *Advertisement*

Dear Dr. Mutt,

It is common knowledge that canines develop 7 times faster than humans, physically and intellectually. Therefore, by the time we have reached 12 months on the human scale, we are actually ready for school; when we are 60 months old, we are eligible to be President of the United States. And by this same calculation, we become senior citizens mighty quickly! So before you know it, you're an old dog, and if you are unprepared for the later years, life can be very miserable. But it doesn't have to be! As a mature hound and founding member of AARC (Allied Association of Retired Canines), let me tell you about a few of the benefits you'll receive as a member of AARC:

- *Bark*, our monthly newsletter, for canine news around the world.
- Discounts on bones and biscuits in your local vet shops.
- Group rate accident insurance with Sniffers Federal Union.
- Invitation to our annual AARC Conference in Dogpatch, NV.

So don't take old age sitting down!
JOIN AARC TODAY!

Retired in Reno

Dear Retired,

Thanks. Please send an application form. You forgot to include it in the envelope with the letter.

I'll pass the information along for the benefit of all.

Sparky

A Hair Raising Experience

Dear Dr. Mutt,

My master is a journalist for a renowned newspaper, and we have spent our adult lives reporting the news around the globe. I can tell you that we have been through many terrifying experiences that would make any sane mutt turn tail and run, but we have survived them all.

Thus, my problem. Lately my fur has grown sparse and thin, and when I pointed this out to my master, his answer was to put me on a vitamin supplement. At first, I smirked at the idea, but after a month on Vitadog Plus, I look like a cotton ball with paws, and I feel like I'm three again!

It's amazing. I only wish that I had been careful with my diet from the beginning, but I won't dwell on the negative. Just let this serve as a warning to all the young folks out there: Enjoy life, but take care of yourself! Exercise and eat right!

Energized in Eureka

Dear Energized,

Stress combined with a diet sorely lacking in basic vitamins and nutrients can turn the furriest canine into a cue ball, and I can imagine what yours would be like always being on the run. Thank your lucky stars that your master is intelligent enough to realize what you need and has the good sense to give it to you. Enjoy your newfound youth!

Sparky

Identity Crisis

Dear Dr. Mutt,

I have six brothers and two sisters, and I don't look like any of them. I never worried about it until the other day when someone came to visit the master. My siblings commenced their hare-brained racket, and I kept to myself as usual. I've gotten used to the ooh's and ah's; but when I heard the words WHAT A CUTE LITTLE KITTY, it was like a dagger to the heart. My hair stood on end and my spine curled automatically. Just imagine, to be called a feline by a total stranger! I was devastated! But that's not the end of the story! Now my mom tells me I'm adopted! She says the master found me in a dumpster and brought me home, and it doesn't matter to her that I'm not a canine because she loves me anyway.

Oh Dr. Mutt, I want to be a dog, but they tell me I'm a cat! What can I do?

Belittled in Baton Rouge

Dear Belittled,

Not to worry whether you are canine or feline, there is room in the world for all of us, and if WE can live together in relative peace and harmony, let the world take note!

The relationship between canines and felines is much maligned, and we do get along with each other much more than advertised. You are a fortunate little feline! You are loved, and that is the sum total of it all. Dare to be different!

Sparky

à la mode

Mon Cher docteur Sparkus,

My name is Fifi, and I am a Parischienne. I was wondering if you 'ave ever been to Paris? You seem like such a debonair dog - so wise and so intelligent. Are you free? If zere is not a Mme Sparkus, you could come to Paris per'aps? Life in Paris is so wonderful. It is beautiful not only in ze springtime. I could show you ze streets!

I would love to meet you!

Enchantée aux Champs Élysés

Dear Fifi,

Alas, there is no Mme Sparkus, and I have never been to Paris anytime! But before I make travel arrangements, maybe we should get to know each other a bit.

I've enclosed a snap of myself. What you see is the real me. So let me know if I should talk to my travel agent.

Sparky

A New Trick for an Old Dog

Dear Friends,

I found this note stuck to Dr. Mutt's keyboard. I guess Fifi must have liked that picture.

Whoever said you can't teach an old dog a new trick never met Sparky. I hope you learned a couple of tricks yourselves! Just remember, it's a dog's life, so you might as well enjoy it!

The Editor

Gone to Paris!
It's Fifi for me!
Be back soon, maybe!

Sparky

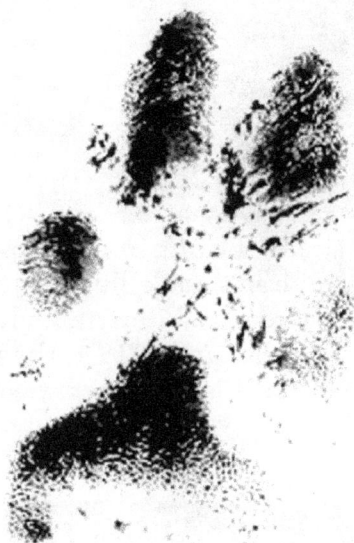

The Illustrator

Andrea Alvarado, the one in the diaper, began her career as a children's book illustrator at a very early age. She wrote and illustrated her first book *The Rabbit and the Little Girl* at the age of three, a short time after this photo was taken.

The Editor

P.V. Alvarado, better known as Pat, was born in the year of the dog so she has always led a dog's life! And she definitely enjoys it!

The Dogtor

Sparkus Tinaquer Mutt was born circa November 1987, somewhere in the Canal Area in the Republic of Panama. As the third puppy in a litter of six full-fledged mutts, Sparkus never knew his dad, but his mom was a trooper. He earned his dogtorate from the Canal Zone Canine College and did his internship as a canine therapist for the pet population in and around the Corozal Vet Clinic.

Sparky, as he is affectionately known, is now semi-retired from chasing garbage trucks and dodging thunder, and dedicates his time to answering letters from disgruntled canines, felines and homo sapiens.